A Happy and Holy Family Lent

GROWING CLOSER TO JESUS

Angela M. Burrin

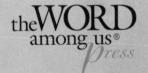

the WORD
among us®
Press

Published by The Word Among Us Press

7115 Guilford Drive, Suite 100

Frederick, Maryland 21704

wau.org

25 24 23 22 21 1 2 3 4 5

ISBN: 978-1-59325-522-0

eISBN: 978-1-59325-523-7

Nihil obstat: The Reverend Michael Morgan, JD, JCL

Censor Librorum

October 27, 2020

Imprimatur: +Most Revered Felipe J. Estévez, STD

Bishop of St. Augustine

October 27, 2020

Design by Suzanne Earl

Made and printed in the United States of America

Library of Congress Control Number:

9781593255220

Contents

Dear Families,

What am I going to give up for Lent? What can I do this Lent? Have you ever asked yourself these questions? I know I do every year! In fact, sometimes Lent can feel like it's all about what we do or what we give up.

This Lent, I would like to invite you to think about how you can grow closer to Jesus. After all, he is the One who gave his life for you, and what better way to have a great Lent than by getting to know him better?

Lent is also the perfect time to spend a little more time together as a family. By spending about fifteen minutes once a week with this booklet, you can experience how simple it can be to grow in your love for God and in knowing his love for you.

Don't let Lent get away from you or overwhelm you this year. I invite you to use this booklet to grow closer to Jesus, to follow him into Holy Week, and to experience the joy of his resurrection on Easter Sunday!

Are you ready to have a happy and holy Lent? I know I am!

Angela

How to Use This Booklet

This booklet is divided into seven sessions—one for each week of Lent, ending with Holy Week and an Easter prayer. You can expect to spend about fifteen minutes with this booklet each week. Additional ideas for activities and prayers are included at the back of the book.

1. Pick a day and time each week that works for you. You might meet around a meal or a snack.

2. Invite God in. You might place a crucifix or light a candle in a central place, and then invite someone to read the opening prayer.

3. Conversation starters. Invite someone to read the first paragraph followed by the conversation starter. This is a fun way for your family to enter into the theme for the week.

4. Story Time. Invite one or two people to read the story. Feel free to stop for conversation if someone has a question or a comment about the story.

5. In Jesus' Time provides an opportunity to learn about daily life while Jesus walked the earth.

6. Jesus, Speak to Me. This passage will help your family to apply the story to your lives.

7. Talk to Jesus. Take a few minutes for each person to think about the main point of the week and to speak with Jesus. Family members may want to share their impressions.

8. Closing Prayer. Invite someone to read the closing prayer.

9. Lenten Activities. Included in this booklet is a variety of Lenten activities for families. You can pick one activity for the whole family (like a Service Saturday) or invite each person to pick their own activity. Also included are two wonderful Lenten practices: the Stations of the Cross and a guide to making a good Confession.

First Week of
Lent

LET US PRAY.

In the name of the **Father** and of the **Son** and of the **Holy Spirit**. Amen.

Jesus, thank you for being with us as we begin our Lenten journey. Help us to experience your love, mercy, and forgiveness in new and unexpected ways. Amen.

Jesus Loves Us

I've lost something!

Have you ever lost something that was very important to you? You may have stopped everything else you were doing to concentrate your time and effort to looking for it. Then when you found it, you might even have told everyone around you, "I found what I lost!"

Take a few minutes to share about when you lost something important and what you had to do to find it.

Jesus, the Good Shepherd

When Jesus taught people about his Father and his heavenly kingdom, he often told stories, called parables, using everyday things to make a point.

He must have been looking out toward some sheep on the hillside when he told this parable. Imagine you are sitting on a rock, listening to Jesus tell this story.

With a smile on his face, Jesus begins:

"Imagine you are a shepherd, and you own a hundred sheep. You are very proud to have so many. Every day, you move the sheep from one place to another so that they will always have plenty of grass to graze on. You do this by calling out to them. The sheep know your voice.

"You love being up on the hillside because it is so peaceful, except when the wolves come to attack your sheep. Then you must yell and make a lot of noise and throw stones to frighten them away.

10

"Because you love your sheep, you count them every day to make sure that you haven't lost any. Then one day you count only ninety-nine sheep. What are you going to do?

"You decide to go looking for that one lost sheep. As you search, you pray that a wild animal hasn't eaten it.

I Know My Sheep

"**S**uddenly you hear a faint bleating. You know that it's your lost sheep. You follow the sound. 'There's my lost sheep!' you cry out. 'Oh no, it's caught in a thornbush.' So you get your crook and carefully lift it out. You put it on your shoulders. Then you walk back to the rest of the flock and gently put it down. You are so happy to have found the sheep that was lost!"

Many people thought Jesus' parable was over, but it wasn't. And what he said made a lot of people in the crowd happy, especially those who knew their lives were not always pleasing to God.

"Wait!" Jesus said. "There's more. I want you know that there is more rejoicing in heaven when one person says to his heavenly Father, 'I am so sorry for the things I've done wrong,' than there is over ninety-nine other people who are already living good lives." Then Jesus said, "I am the Good Shepherd. I know my sheep and my sheep know me."

Jesus, Speak to Me

Just as a shepherd makes sure that his sheep are safe and protected, I want to help you stay close to me so that you will be safe. I want to protect you from places, people, and things that will take you away from me.

One way to stay close to me is to talk to me during your day. I love it when you say, "Good morning, Jesus" when you wake up or "Hello, Jesus" when you pass by a church.

Talk to Jesus

In your mind, tell Jesus one way you want to stay close to him this week.

LET US PRAY.

Jesus, thank you for reminding us that we are so special to you and that you are our Good Shepherd. During this first week of Lent, help us to remember that you love everyone in our family very much.

In the name of the **Father** and of the **Son** and of the **Holy Spirit**. Amen.

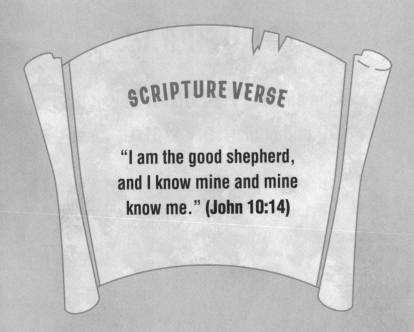

SCRIPTURE VERSE

"I am the good shepherd, and I know mine and mine know me." (John 10:14)

Second Week of
Lent

LET US PRAY.

In the name of the **Father** and of the **Son** and of the **Holy Spirit**. Amen.

Father, thank you for being with us. Open our minds to receive what you have in store for us. Amen.

Jesus Is Always with Us

There's going to be a storm!

There are some signs of when a storm is about to hit: dark clouds roll in, the wind begins to get stronger, the temperature drops, the thunder rumbles, lightning flashes, birds and animals take shelter, raindrops begin to fall, and outdoor sports games are stopped.

Jesus Sleeps during the Storm

Take a few minutes to share about when you had to take precautions when a storm was coming.

After a long day of teaching the crowds and healing many people, Jesus was tired. He asked Peter,

"Will you row me out to the middle of the lake in your boat so that I can get away from the crowds and sleep for a few hours?" Peter replied, "Of course, Jesus. Jump in." Some of Jesus' disciples joined them.

Jesus went to the back of the boat and quickly fell asleep on a cushion. The wind that evening was strong and quickly carried the fishing boat into the middle of the lake. Then suddenly, almost out of nowhere, dark rain clouds began to move across the sky right towards the boat.

Philip said nervously to Peter, "We are going to have a big storm. Let's cover Jesus with my cloak so he won't get wet." No sooner had he done that than heavy rain started to drench everyone.

IN JESUS' TIME

Jesus spent much time near the Sea of Galilee. At some places, the lake is so wide that you can't even see land on the other side. The lake can also be a dangerous place for fishermen because fierce winds and violent storms often happen suddenly, without any warning.

Not only was it raining hard, but the winds were getting strong and stronger. As one huge wave after another splashed into the boat, the disciples began to yell and scream, "We're going to sink!" They all held onto their seats so that they wouldn't be tossed out into the water. Surprisingly, Jesus didn't wake up.

"Why Were You So Afraid?"

No one knew what to do. Then Peter started crawling towards the back of the boat towards Jesus. When he reached Jesus, he shook him and said, "Jesus, help us! We are about to drown."

Jesus knew that all his friends were frightened. He got to his feet, told the wind to die down, and said to the sea, "Peace! Be still!"

Immediately, the water became calm. The dark clouds were blown away by a gentle breeze. Jesus looked at his disciples and said, "Why were you so afraid? Have you still no faith?"

Jesus, Speak to Me

I asked my disciples why they had no faith. I was with them, and instead of being nervous, they could have trusted in me. But often it is hard to stay calm when you feel anxious. Adults and children all struggle with fear sometimes, but it can keep you from doing important things for me.

Remember: I am near you when you are worried about something. The next time you feel nervous, say my name—*Jesus*. Imagine me standing next to you, holding your hand. I'm right there with you.

Talk to Jesus

In your mind, tell Jesus what you are worried about. He's listening to you.

LET US PRAY.

Jesus, it is so comforting to know you are always with us, even when we're going through a difficult time. This week, help us to turn to you and to remind one another that you are always with us.

In the name of the **Father** and of the **Son** and of the **Holy Spirit**. Amen.

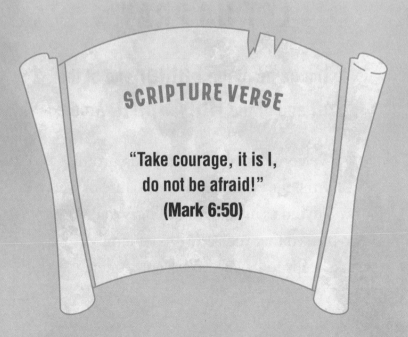

SCRIPTURE VERSE

"Take courage, it is I,
do not be afraid!"
(Mark 6:50)

Third Week of Lent

LET US PRAY.

In the name of the **Father** and of the **Son** and of the **Holy Spirit**. Amen.

Welcome, Holy Spirit. Jesus promised that he would send the Counselor who would lead us into all truth. That's you! We're so blessed that you are with our family as we take steps to have a holy Lent. Amen.

Jesus Invites Us to Be Generous

Getting Directions

Cities, towns, and large parks often have guided walks. The path is clearly marked and could include maps, historical data, or scenic overlooks. Using the GPS on phones on a walk is another option to get from A to B. Without either of these, there's always the chance of getting lost or going into an unsafe area.

Take a few minutes to share about a time when you went on a drive or a hike and used a GPS.

Who Is My Neighbor?

Many people followed Jesus to listen to his teaching. But not everyone liked what he said, and some people even tried to trick him. One day, someone asked Jesus, "How can I please God and go to heaven when I die?"

Jesus replied, "That's a very good question. What you need to do is to love God and love your neighbor." Then the man asked, "And who is my neighbor?" Jesus then said, "I'll tell you a story that will answer your question."

IN JESUS' TIME

In Jesus' time, people walked everywhere: to work, to the market, to the well, to places of worship, and to visit family and friends. For a long journey, they might travel by donkey, mule, horse, or camel. There were sometimes rivers to cross and the danger of robbers hiding behind rocks.

"Early one morning a man left Jerusalem on a journey to Jericho. He wore his best tunic, cloak, and sandals. Two money bags hung on the leather belt around his waist. After walking over some hills, the man saw a stream. 'Oh, I can't wait for a cool drink of water,' he thought. He started off down the rocky, dusty path to the stream. There was no one else around—or so he thought.

"Suddenly, four robbers jumped out from behind a rock. They knocked him to the ground and beat him so badly that he couldn't move. Then they took his bags of money and his new clothes and ran away.

An Unexpected Friend

"The injured man lay in the hot sun for a long time. All he could do was pray that someone would come along to help him. Finally, he heard footsteps. He looked up and saw a priest from the Temple in his fine clothes coming toward him. 'Great! This priest will help me,' he thought. But guess what? The priest was busy reading his prayers and didn't stop to help him.

"Sometime later the man heard someone singing praises to God. 'What beautiful singing! That must be a Levite from the Temple. I'm sure he'll stop and help me,' the man thought. He tried to call for help, but he was too weak to speak. Did the Levite see the injured man? Yes! But he pretended that he didn't, and he walked over to the other side of the road.

"'Won't anyone help me?' the man sobbed. Suddenly, along the path came a stranger riding on a donkey. 'Oh no, it's a Samaritan. He won't help me. He's one of our enemies,' the man thought to himself. So he was really surprised when the Samaritan came over to him and said, 'It looks like you need help.' The Samaritan got off his donkey. Very gently, he cleansed and soothed the injured man's wounds with wine and olive oil and then wrapped his cuts and bruises in bandages. Then he gave the man a long, cool drink from his water flask.

"'I can't leave you here,' said the Samaritan. 'I'm going to put you on my donkey and take you to an inn in Jericho.' When they got to the inn, the Samaritan said to the owner, 'This man has been attacked by robbers. He's injured. Here's money for him to stay in one of your rooms until he's better. If that's not enough, I'll give you more when I return.'"

After Jesus had finished the story, he asked, "Which of those three men was a good neighbor to the man who was injured?" The man who had asked Jesus the question replied, "The one who stopped and helped the man." Jesus looked at him and said, "You're right. Now go and be a good neighbor too."

Jesus, Speak to Me

The priest and the Levite were so wrapped up in their own lives that they didn't stop to help the injured man. Like them, sometimes people can be so wrapped up in their own concerns that

they are not aware of someone else's need. Or they may feel too busy to help or be afraid of getting involved.

The Good Samaritan was happy to help even though it cost him time and money.

This week, look for opportunities to be a Good Samaritan. A smile, a hello, or a "How are you?" can show someone that you care about them.

Talk to Jesus

In your mind, tell Jesus you are sorry for the times when you have not helped someone in need. Receive his forgiveness and his encouragement to help others when they are in need.

LET US PRAY.

Holy Spirit, you are so faithful in showing us how we can be more loving and kind and how by our prayer and actions we can bring God's kingdom of love, peace, and joy into our world. This week, help us to see that each person is so special and deserving of our attention, time, and care.

In the name of the Father and of the Son and of the Holy Spirit. Amen.

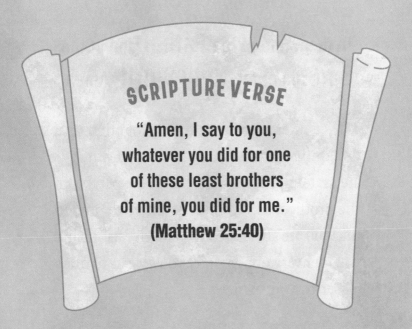

SCRIPTURE VERSE

"Amen, I say to you, whatever you did for one of these least brothers of mine, you did for me."
(Matthew 25:40)

Fourth Week of Lent

LET US PRAY.

In the name of the **Father** and of the **Son** and of the **Holy Spirit**. Amen.

Jesus, here we are, coming together as a family for this fourth week of Lent. We are grateful that, as we focus on the parable of the prodigal son, we will again be reminded that you are always ready to forgive us. Thank you for every opportunity you give us to draw closer to you. Amen.

Jesus Forgives Us

Behind the Scenes

It is easy to take many things in life for granted. Take, for example, our food items. Most of us go to the grocery store, put items in a cart, pay, and bring them home. But do you ever think about how much work goes into producing a loaf of bread, a box of mac and cheese, a can of beans, or a bottle of orange juice?

Take a few minutes to share about what might have been involved in putting one of your favorite food items together before it arrived at the grocery store.

A Boy Looks for Happiness

"Once there was a rich farmer who had two sons. Both sons worked on their father's farm. The older son was a good worker and did everything that his father asked him to do. But the younger son wasn't very happy. He kept complaining, 'I don't like doing all this hard work. I want to go away and have some fun.' Then he had an idea. He went into the house and asked, 'Father, would you give me my share of the money that will be mine one day?' His father was sad, but he replied, 'Son, if that is what you want, here it is.'

IN JESUS' TIME

As Jesus and his disciples walked from one town to another, they would often pass through fields of wheat, millet, oats, and barley. They would see the farmer and his sons or hired men preparing the soil for planting using a wooden plough pulled by oxen. When the time came for harvesting the crops, they would use a sickle to cut the crops and then tie them into sheaves.

"Oh, the younger son was so happy! He quickly got together a few of his things, and off he went. After days of walking, he arrived in a nearby new country. He said to himself, 'This is going to be so exciting!' He bought some new clothes. Then he went to the market and spent lots of his money on food and drink and threw a big party for his friends. Everyone knew that this stranger had a lot of money. 'We really like you,' they said. 'Can we come here for another party tomorrow?' Every day he went out and spent more and more of his money.

"One day when the younger son counted his money, he found that he only had enough left to buy a loaf of bread. He went to his new friends and said, 'I've invited you to many meals at my house. Now that I have no money left, may I come to your house?' 'No!' they replied. 'Go away. We don't want to be your friends anymore.' So he went away. That day he only had bread to eat. The next day, he had nothing to eat, but again, his friends refused to give him anything. He decided to find a job. He asked many people if they would give him work.

Happiness Is with the Father

"At last a farmer told the younger son that he could take care of the pigs. It was a very dirty job, and he didn't like it. But at least he had something to eat. Can you guess what he ate? The pigs' food! One day when he was cleaning out the pigpen, he thought, 'What am I doing here? I'm really sad and lonely. I want to go home.' So he decided to go back home. On the way he thought about what he would say to his father: 'Father, I'm sorry for leaving you. I've done many wrong things since I left home. I

want to come back. But I don't deserve to be your son anymore. I will be one of your servants.'

"All the time that the young son was away, his father had missed him very much. Every day he would look toward the road, hoping to see him returning. Then one day, in the distance, the father spotted someone walking toward him. 'Could this be my son?' he wondered. 'It is!' he exclaimed. He ran toward his son and hugged him and kissed him. He was very, very happy to see him again.

"The son said, 'Father, forgive me. Let me come back and be one of your servants.' But instead of answering him, the father called out, 'Servants, go and get new clothes and sandals for my son! Bring one of my golden rings. Let's have a party to celebrate. My Son has come back to me!'"

Jesus, Speak to Me

Close your eyes, and imagine the father in this parable running out to his younger son and giving him a big hug! Now open your eyes. Just like that father, I want you to know that my heavenly Father is thrilled whenever anyone says to him, "Father, I have done wrong; please forgive me."

You can do this when you say your night prayers. This is how: Take a few minutes to look back over your day and recall the good things that happened and also those things that you know in your heart and mind were not right. For the things you are sorry for, ask forgiveness in your own words, or, if you know it, say an Act of Contrition. Then, go peacefully to sleep, and awake refreshed to live another new day for me!

Talk to the Father

In your mind, thank your heavenly Father for being loving and forgiving and for calling you his special son or daughter.

LET US PRAY.

Father, your mercy, forgiveness, and unconditional love are truly wonderful graces! Help us as a family to grow in forgiveness—forgiving ourselves, forgiving others, and receiving your forgiveness. This is a real way to make Lent a happy and holy time.

In the name of the **Father** and of the **Son** and of the **Holy Spirit**. Amen.

SCRIPTURE VERSE

"This son of mine was dead, and has come to life again; he was lost, and has been found." (Luke 15:24)

Fifth Week of
Lent

LET US PRAY.

In the name of the **Father** and of the **Son** and of the **Holy Spirit**. Amen.

Jesus, you always wanted to please your Father by doing what he asked of you. We were on your mind as you began your terrible suffering. We want to draw close to you again during this family time by reflecting on the last days of your life. Amen.

Jesus Suffered for Us

It's Time for Church

One of the beautiful things that families do together on Sundays is go to Mass. Jesus is waiting for us to say, "Hello, Jesus" to him in the tabernacle. He always enjoys hearing us sing hymns, say prayers, and talk to him in our hearts. And of course, Jesus longs for us to receive him in the Eucharist!

Take a few minutes to share about some of the parish activities that you most enjoy.

Jesus Is Betrayed

After he had celebrated the feast of the Passover with his disciples, Jesus took his disciples to the Garden of Gethsemane. There, Judas betrayed Jesus. Jesus was arrested by soldiers and taken to the house of Caiaphas the high priest. At the same time, scribes and elders of the Temple as well as members of the Sanhedrin—the powerful Jewish council—were also heading towards the house.

After questioning Jesus, Caiaphas ordered him to be taken to the praetorium, the home of Pilate, the Roman governor. Crowds were gathered in the courtyard waiting for Pilate to come out from the judgment hall. Someone in the crowd said, "The chief priests are accusing Jesus of making himself a king and telling the people not to pay taxes to Caesar. But Pilate doesn't think Jesus deserves to die."

When Pilate appeared, the crowd became quiet. Pilate said, "I don't think this man has done anything wrong. But every year at Passover, I release a criminal. Whom shall I release this year? Do you want me to release Jesus or the murderer Barabbas?" While some shouted "Jesus," most of the crowd cried out, "Barabbas, Barabbas, Barabbas!" Pilate was shocked, but wanting to please the people, he said, "What shall I do with Jesus of Nazareth?" The air filled with shouts of "Crucify him! Crucify him!" So Jesus was sentenced to death.

Jesus Begins His Suffering

Several soldiers led Jesus into the courtyard. They took off his clothing and tied him to a pole. Then they took turns striking Jesus with leather whips that had bits of bone tied to the ends. A

solder said, "How many times have we struck him?" One answered, "Thirty-nine, and this one will make it forty." Jesus was bleeding all over his shoulders, back, arms, and legs. He was in excruciating pain, but he didn't cry out or complain.

Some other soldiers were watching as Jesus was whipped. "He said he was a king; how can we make him look like a king?" one of them asked. "He needs a royal robe!" They found a robe and placed it over his bleeding shoulders. "Now he needs a crown," mocked another soldier. He searched for branches with large thorns and twisted them into a crown. "Look what I have for you, Jesus," he said mockingly as he pushed the crown of thorns into Jesus' head.

All the soldiers started laughing at Jesus. Some got on their knees before him and said, "Hail, king of the Jews!" Others were spitting at him. When they had finished making fun of Jesus, they led him away to be crucified.

Jesus, Speak to Me

I was in great pain after the lashes I received. The soldiers hurt me by their actions, but when they made fun of me, I was also hurt by their words. It's easy to hurt others with careless words. Everyone is a child of God, created in his image and likeness. It disappoints me when my Father's children insult or say cruel things about one another. Please try to speak to everyone, as well as about everyone, with kindness.

Think for a moment about my Father's great love. He loves you so much that he was willing to let me suffer in many ways, including being made fun of. This was all part of my Father's great plan to bring all his sons and daughters back into friendship with him. Always remember that!

Talk to the Holy Spirit

In your mind, ask the Holy Spirit to fill your heart with kindness and to help you to use your tongue to say nice things about those in your life—especially the people in your family.

LET US PRAY.

Jesus, thank you for accepting all the insults and physical pain for us. You even forgave the soldiers who were so cruel to you. Jesus, our family wants to say aloud to you, "Jesus, thank you for suffering for us." Amen.

In the name of the **Father** and of the **Son** and of the **Holy Spirit**. Amen.

SCRIPTURE VERSE

Love is patient, love is kind.
It is not jealous, [love] is
not pompous, it is not inflated.
(1 Corinthians 13:4)

Sixth Week of
Lent

LET US PRAY.

In the name of the **Father** and of the **Son** and of the **Holy Spirit**. Amen.

Jesus, how you love everyone in our family! You love us just as much as you loved the men you chose to be your apostles. Whenever they did something wrong, you corrected them in love. Thank you for giving us the Holy Spirit to show us the truth. Amen.

Jesus Helps Us Tell the Truth

Seeing in the Dark

Sometimes our homes lose power, and if it happens at night, it can get very dark! Then we use flashlights or candles so that we can see. In the animal world, God has made certain animals able to see in the dark: moths, bats, raccoons, opossums, red foxes, and some monkeys.

Take a few minutes to share about when your home lost power or when you needed to use a flashlight to find something in a dark place.

Peter Follows Jesus

Jesus was arrested in the middle of the night. As it was dark, Peter was able to follow Jesus without being noticed as he was taken to the home of Caiaphas. Peter said to himself, "I must stay close to Jesus and find out what's going to happen to him. I just don't understand why people think that he's dangerous." Then fear filled his heart as he thought, "What will they decide to do to Jesus? All I know is I can't leave Jesus. Not now, not ever."

As he got through the gate of Caiaphas' house, Peter walked around the sides of the courtyard so as not to be seen or questioned about why he was there. It was a cold night, and some soldiers had lit a fire to keep themselves warm. Being tired and anxious made the night seem even colder, so Peter moved closer to the fire. As he got closer, one of the servant girls saw his face in the light. "I've seen you before," she said. "You have traveled with the man inside: Jesus of Nazareth." Peter quickly answered with the first thing that came to his mind: "I don't know what you're talking about."

Relieved that the servant girl didn't ask any more questions, Peter moved away from the fire and sat down under a window outside the place where Jesus was being questioned. Suddenly, another servant
girl recognized Peter. She said,

IN JESUS' TIME

In order to have light when it was dark, lanterns filled with olive oil were put on a shelf or table. Only a few lanterns were needed as most homes were only the size of one or two rooms. Houses were often made of mud and brick with small slits for window. The roof was flat made of wooden beams covered with straw and clay. Food was cooked over an open fire either in the home or outside.

"I've seen you with Jesus of Nazareth." Again, without thinking, Peter replied, "I swear I don't know the man."

Peter Betrays Jesus

Afraid of any more questions, Peter got up and started walking towards the corner of the courtyard. But he didn't get far before someone said, "Hey! I'm sure you are one of that man's disciples. I heard you answer that servant girl. You even talk like that man Jesus. Yes! Your accent is from Galilee. That's where he's from. You must know him." Peter was scared and angry. "I've told you, I don't know the man," he said.

Just then the rooster crowed. Peter remembered what Jesus had said: "Peter, before the rooster crows, you will deny knowing me three times." Peter was devastated. He said to himself, "I boasted to Jesus that I would never deny him, but I did! Why did I say I didn't know him? Why couldn't I have said, 'Yes, of course I know him. I'm one of his closest friends.' Why was I such a coward?"

Peter ran out of the courtyard and into the street, sobbing and saying, "Jesus, I'm so sorry. Jesus, forgive me."

Jesus, Speak to Me

I know that Peter really loved me. He had left everything to follow me. But when it came time for a big test, he failed it. He lied. It wasn't that he didn't love me, but he was afraid that if he told the truth about knowing me, he might be arrested or punished.

Are there times when you have lied because you were afraid of getting punished? The next time you are tempted to lie, ask the Holy Spirit to give you the courage to be honest.

After Peter received my Holy Spirit at Pentecost, he was a changed man! With the help of the Holy Spirit, he was never afraid again to tell people that he knew me. In fact, thanks to Peter, thousands of people came to believe that I was their Savior!

Talk to Jesus

In your mind, ask Jesus to forgive you for the times when you've told lies or things that weren't the whole truth.

LET US PRAY.

Holy Spirit, you are so kind when you correct us. We know more and more in our hearts that our Father is always ready to forgive us, just as he forgave Peter for denying knowing Jesus. This week as a family, help us to be more open and honest with one other. Amen.

In the name of the **Father** and of the **Son** and of the **Holy Spirit**. Amen.

SCRIPTURE VERSE

"The truth will set you free."
(John 8:32)

Holy Week of
Lent

LET US PRAY.

In the name of the **Father** and of the **Son** and of the **Holy Spirit**. Amen.

Father, thank you for caring for our family as we come together to reflect on the final hours of Jesus' life. You and the Holy Spirit saw from heaven everything that happened to Jesus. Together with Mary our Mother, we want to be with Jesus as he is stripped of his outer garments and nailed to the cross. Amen.

Jesus Dies for Us

That's Too Hard!

There are some things that are hard for us to do. It might be that we don't have the skill (like riding a bike), we don't know how to begin (like cleaning a room), or emotionally it's too demanding (like forgiving someone who hurt us). We might say, "That's too hard!"

Simon of Cyrene Helps Jesus Carry His Cross

The midmorning air was hot and humid as Jesus—who had taught the crowds

Take a few minutes to share about when you were able to do something that you thought at first would be too hard to do.

about the Father's love—came out of the courtyard of the praetorium struggling under the weight of a large wooden cross. He
dragged the cross along the narrow stone streets towards the city
gate and then up the rocky hill of execution, called Calvary. What
an agonizing walk of almost one third of a mile!

Along the way, Jesus fell three times under the weight of the
cross. His mother, Mary, saw it all. She was grateful when Simon
of Cyrene began to help her son. But her heart was broken see-
ing Jesus suffering and blood from the crown of thorns trickling
down his face.

IN JESUS' TIME

For washing and cooking, water
had to be drawn from a well and
carried home in large jars, often
carefully balanced on heads.
Breads and cakes were made from
grain that had been ground between
two millstones. Clothes were from
wool sheared from local sheep
or linen from flaxseed harvested
from the fields. Both were long but
rewarding processes.

Once Jesus reached the top of Calvary, the soldiers took the cross
from Simon of Cyrene. Mary and Jesus' disciple John stood on
the hill.

The cries of two criminals who were being nailed to their crosses
could be heard. The whole crowd became very quiet. A soldier
gave Jesus a mug of cheap wine, but Jesus refused to drink it.

"Come on! Let's get this one ready for crucifixion," one of the
solders called out. Two soldiers ripped off Jesus' cloak. Jesus was
now naked except for a loincloth.

Just as Jesus was about to fall again, the soldiers grabbed him
and led him to his cross, which was lying on the ground. They
pushed him down backwards onto the cross. His bruised body
hit the wood hard.

Jesus Is Crucified

Four soldiers stretched out his arms and legs to match them up with the holes in the wood. A large wooden nail was hammered into each of his hands, and one through both of his feet. Then they lifted the heavy cross on which hung Jesus, the Savior of the world. It swayed as it was dropped into a deep hole.

The crowd watching the crucifixion began to mock and jeer at Jesus. Someone said, "If he was able to perform so many wondrous

miracles, why doesn't he just get off the cross?" Another shouted at Jesus, "You who would destroy the Temple and rebuild it in three days, save yourself and come down from the cross!" Others said, "Let the Messiah, the king of Israel, come down from the cross so that we may see and believe!"

Off to the side of the crucifixion, soldiers divided Jesus' clothes equally between them. But because his cloak was made from a single piece of woven material, they decided to roll some dice to see which of them would get it. The winner got the whole cloak.

Pilate had an inscription written and ordered it to be placed on the cross over Jesus' head. It read, "Jesus of Nazareth, the King of the Jews." The Jewish leaders didn't like it. One complained that the plaque should have said, "This man claimed to be the King of the Jews." But Pilate wouldn't listen to them and said, "What I have written, I have written."

Jesus was between the crosses of the two criminals who were also crucified that day. One of the criminals asked Jesus, "Aren't you the Messiah? Then save yourself and us." "Don't say that," rebuked the other criminal. "We have done wrong. We deserve to die. But this man has done nothing wrong." Turning to Jesus, he said, "Jesus, remember me when you come into your kingdom." Jesus said, "I want you to know that today you will be with me in paradise."

Then Jesus said, "It is finished," and he bowed his head and died.

Jesus, Speak to Me

As the nails were being hammered into my hands and feet, I knew that I was doing my Father's will.

I willingly took your sins upon myself and became the perfect, unblemished sacrificial Lamb, just like the lamb the high priest would offer at Passover. I redeemed you. Yes, all your sins were washed away with my blood, even those that you might think are too big for me to forgive. So rejoice in my great love for you.

Today I ask you to forgive anyone who has hurt you in any way. Please don't hold any grudges. Remember that I have forgiven all your sins. So forgive as you have been forgiven. Look into your heart now to see if there is anyone that you need to forgive.

Talk to Jesus

In your mind, ask Jesus to give you the strength to forgive anyone who has hurt you, even if you don't think they deserve your forgiveness.

LET US PRAY.

Jesus, thank you for your sacrifice on the cross. This week, help us to remember how much you love us and the price that you paid for the forgiveness of our sins. Amen.

In the name of the **Father** and of the **Son** and of the **Holy Spirit**. Amen.

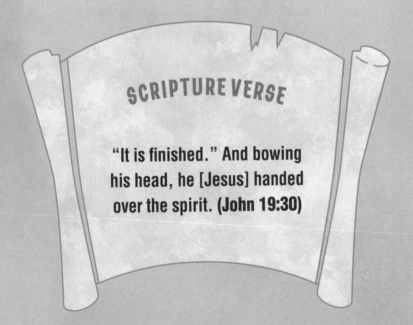

SCRIPTURE VERSE

"It is finished." And bowing his head, he [Jesus] handed over the spirit. (John 19:30)

EASTER SUNDAY

A Resurrection Day Prayer

Three days after Jesus' death and burial, something
amazing happened.
Christ is risen. Alleluia!

An angel of the Lord rolled back the stone.
Christ is risen. Alleluia!

Jesus rose from the dead.
Christ is risen. Alleluia!

Jesus is the resurrection and the life.
Christ is risen. Alleluia!

Jesus appeared first to Mary Magdalene.
Christ is risen. Alleluia!

Peter and John ran to the tomb—but it was empty.
Christ is risen. Alleluia!

Jesus appeared to two disciples on the road to Emmaus.
Christ is risen. Alleluia!

Jesus helped his disciples to have a miraculous
catch of fish.
Christ is risen. Alleluia!

Jesus told Thomas to believe by putting his hand
in his wounds and side.
Christ is risen. Alleluia!

After forty days Jesus ascended to our Father in heaven.
Christ is risen. Alleluia!

On the feast of Pentecost, Jesus sent us the Holy Spirit.
Christ is risen. Alleluia!

Jesus is with us and never leaves us.
Christ is risen. Alleluia!

The Stations of the Cross

The Stations of the Cross are one of the most popular and treasured traditions in the Catholic faith. This devotion will bring you closer to Jesus as you remember all that he has done for you.

1. Jesus is condemned to death. Jesus was accused of many crimes he didn't commit. He didn't defend himself. He was willing to die for our sins.

For the sake of his sorrowful passion, have mercy on us and on the whole world.

2. Jesus accepts the cross. The cross was big and heavy. It was hard for Jesus to carry it. Jesus carried the cross without complaining.

For the sake of his sorrowful passion, have mercy on us and on the whole world.

3. Jesus falls the first time. Jesus was already in a lot of pain when he fell the first time. It must have hurt very much. Jesus got up and kept on going.

For the sake of his sorrowful passion, have mercy on us and on the whole world.

4. Jesus meets his mother. Jesus knew that his mother, Mary, was sad to see him suffering so much. But he was comforted to have her near him.

For the sake of his sorrowful passion, have mercy on us and on the whole world.

5. Simon of Cyrene helps Jesus. Simon didn't come to help Jesus but to see what was going on. Then he was ordered by the soldiers to carry the cross because Jesus was having such a hard time.

For the sake of his sorrowful passion, have mercy on us and on the whole world.

6. Veronica wipes Jesus' face. When Veronica saw the blood trickling down from the crown of thorns onto Jesus' face, she wanted to help him. She risked getting in trouble from the soldiers as she gently wiped his face, but her kindness overcame her fear.

For the sake of his sorrowful passion, have mercy on us and on the whole world.

7. Jesus falls a second time. Jesus fell again because he was so weak and tired. He struggled to his feet and continued on.

For the sake of his sorrowful passion, have mercy on us and on the whole world.

8. Jesus meets the women of Jerusalem. A lot of people were against Jesus, but a lot of people followed him. They were his faithful friends.

For the sake of his sorrowful passion, have mercy on us and on the whole world.

9. Jesus falls a third time. It's unbelievable that Jesus fell again and that the soldiers didn't help him. They only yelled louder for him to get up and keep walking.

For the sake of his sorrowful passion, have mercy on us and on the whole world.

10. Jesus is stripped of his clothes. As the soldiers took off his garments, Jesus experienced more pain. He was comforted knowing his Father in heaven loved him and had not abandoned him.

For the sake of his sorrowful passion, have mercy on us and on the whole world.

11. Jesus is crucified. The soldiers drove nails through Jesus' hands and feet. They lifted up the cross and put it in place. Jesus was in agony.

For the sake of his sorrowful passion, have mercy on us and on the whole world.

12. Jesus dies on the cross. When Jesus died, the sky got dark, and the ground started to shake. This made some people very scared. They realized that Jesus was innocent and that they had made a big mistake.

For the sake of his sorrowful passion, have mercy on us and on the whole world.

13. Jesus' body is taken down from the cross. Joseph of Arimathea gave Jesus his own burial cave. Joseph was another one of Jesus' friends who took a risk to help him.

For the sake of his sorrowful passion, have mercy on us and on the whole world.

14. Jesus is laid in the tomb. Even when things look very difficult and sad, there is always hope that God can bring new life.

For the sake of his sorrowful passion, have mercy on us and on the whole world.

Lenten Activities

Below are some suggested ways to help you and your family have a happy and holy Lent and to grow closer to Jesus. Choose one or two that will be especially meaningful for your family.

Lenten Candles

If your family enjoys Advent wreaths, set up seven candles in the shape of a cross to mark the weeks of Lent. Use purple candles for each week of Lent, but put a white one in the center or at the top for Easter Sunday.

Cross for Christ

On Ash Wednesday, make a big cross out of poster board, and hang it in your kitchen or family room. Then cut out several dozen smaller crosses from construction paper, and keep them nearby. Whenever a family member does something special for Jesus, he or she can tape a small cross to the big one. See how many little crosses your family joins with Jesus' cross during Lent!

Be a "Secret Simon" of Cyrene

Put the names of all the members of your family into a bag. Each week during the family Lenten prayer time, have everyone draw a name and keep it a secret. Every day that week, try to do something kind for that person, without letting him or her know who did it. One day you might write a note of encouragement before a test,

draw a picture, or secretly perform a household chore. Try to keep one another's secrets for the week, even if you catch on. Then, at the end of the week, you can each try to guess who your "Secret Simon" was.

Soup Suppers

Prepare a simple soup one night a week, and deposit the money that you would have spent on dinner in the poor box at your church or donate it to a charity. You may want to join other families in this practice or check out local parishes to see if they offer Lent soup suppers.

Stations of the Cross

For younger children, draw your own stations on construction paper. Place them around the house. One evening after dinner, visit some of the stations as a family. Try to attend the Stations of the Cross at your parish several times during Lent.

Pray the Sorrowful Mysteries of the Rosary

This is one of the most significant ways of reflecting on Jesus' suffering and death. To enhance the meaning of those events, find a scriptural rosary booklet in your local Catholic bookstore (or online), and read the verses for that mystery before each Hail Mary.

Pretzel Making

In the days of the very strict Lenten fasts, pretzels made from flour, water, and yeast were a staple food. They were shaped in the form of a person's arms crossed in prayer. Make homemade pretzels. Your kids will love rolling out the

dough into pretzels—and eating them. Suggested recipe can be found online.

Puppet Show

Choose a story from this booklet, and put on a puppet show. Make simple puppets out of paper lunch bags, or draw pictures and staple them to ice-pop sticks. Have the children hide behind your sofa and act out the story with their puppets.

Make a Pilgrimage

Is there a nearby shrine, monastery, or cathedral that you could visit? As part of your trip, explore the local history, and pray together as a family. Stop for lunch afterward.

Activities for Holy Week

Make the Easter Triduum—Holy Thursday through Holy Saturday—a special family time. These are "holy" days in the original sense of the word—days set apart to pray and fast in anticipation of the glory of Easter morning. Plan to go as a family, if possible, to the Holy Thursday and Good Friday services at your parish.

Christian Seder Meal

Learn about the seder meal online, and see how you can do a simplified seder meal with your family on Holy Thursday. You might add an ingredient to your dinner, such as roasted lamb, unleavened bread, or bitter herbs, or say a simple prayer together.

Experience the Passion as a Family

On Good Friday, read the Gospel account of Jesus' passion as a family. Assign parts to members of the family who are old enough to participate. Or watch a movie depicting the life and death of Jesus.

Making a Good Confession

If you have made your first confession, come to Jesus this Lent in the Sacrament of Reconciliation. He is waiting for you. A simply way to prepare for Confession is to take a few minutes to look back over the time since your last confession. Thank Jesus for the good things that happened or the kind things you were able to do. If you remember something that you did that wasn't right or that was unkind or hurtful, these are the things to mention in Confession.

If it's been a long time since your last confession, the priest will help you to make it a good one. Jesus is always ready to forgive you and to give you his peace of knowing that your sins are forgiven.

On the way home from Confession, you might want to share how you felt when the priest said, "I absolve you from your sins, in the name of the Father, Son, and Holy Spirit. Go in peace; your sins are forgiven." Did you know that the angels rejoice for all those whose sins have been forgiven? You might even celebrate your forgiveness with a treat!

Act of Contrition

My God,
I am sorry for my sins with all my heart.
In choosing to do wrong
and failing to do good,
I have sinned against you
whom I should love above all things.
I firmly intend, with your help,
to do penance,
to sin no more,
and to avoid whatever leads me to sin.
Our Savior Jesus Christ suffered and died for us.
In his name, my God, have mercy.

Fifty Days of Celebration

The Easter season is so important that the Church sets aside fifty days to celebrate Jesus' victory over sin and death—all the way to Pentecost!

Here are some easy suggestions for your family to continue rejoicing long after the last jelly bean is gone. Just pick a few ideas that work for you and your family.

1. Use a special candle at family meals to recall the light of Christ.

2. Use the old Easter greeting and response: "Christ is risen! – He is risen indeed!"

3. Put up a sign or banner that proclaims, "He is risen!"

4. Add an Easter prayer—or an "Alleluia"—to your grace before meals. (See page 72 for an idea.)

5. Drape your crucifixes and crosses with a strip of white cloth.

6. Make cookies in the shapes of Easter symbols. Freeze some to serve throughout the season.

7. Have a family time of reading together from the Easter story: Matthew 28, Mark 16, Luke 24, or John 20-21.

8. Make a poster of a life-giving cross. Add paper flowers and leaves to it throughout Easter.

9. The Sunday after Easter is Divine Mercy Sunday. Explore this beautiful devotion (thedivinemercy.org).

10. Was anyone received into the Church during your parish Easter Vigil? Have them over or send them a welcome card.

11. Keep fresh flowers around.

12. Talk about Baptism. Tell stories of family members' Baptisms.

13. Use a special container for newly blessed water from church. Show younger children how to bless themselves with the holy water.

14. Learn how other cultures celebrate Easter. Try out some of their customs and foods.

15. Listen to Handel's Messiah and other Easter music.

16. Read about the Emmaus disciples (Luke 24:13-35); take a family walk.

17. Celebrate new life by doing something as a family to support unborn children and their parents.

18. Plant some seeds and watch for signs of life.

A Prayer for Every Day of the Easter Season

This is the day the Lord has made.
   Let us rejoice and be glad today!
You are my God, and I will thank you.
   You are my God, and I will praise your
     greatness. (Psalm 118:24, 28, ICB)
Jesus, you have risen from the dead and
   overcome sin and death!
You have opened heaven for us and made
   all things new.
Together we rejoice in your unending
   love for us!
Alleluia!